Olivia's Pod

An Orca's Tale

KURT MEIDINGER

EDITORS
Debby Alten
Sandra Schoger Foster

PHOTOGRAPHS
Special thanks to NOAA (National Oceanic and Atmospheric Administration) for permission to use their photographs.

pg. i Credit: Robert L. Pitman
pg. v Credit: Jeff Hogan / NOAA
pg. vii Credit: Candace Emmons / NWFSC /NOAA

pg. 1, 10, 22, 28, Credit: Robert L. Pitman / NOAA
pg. 3, 4, 16, 27, Credit: NOAA
pg. 5, Credit: Rear Admiral Harley D. Nygren / NOAA Corps (ret.)
pg. 6, Credit: Joshua Keaton / NOAA
pg. 8, Credit: Dr. Brandon Southall / NOAA, NMFS/OPR
pg. 13, Transient Orca with Harbor Porpoise: © Robin W. Baird
pg. 14, Credit: Melanie Johnson / NOAA/NMFS/NWFSC
pg. 15, Credit: Ed Bowlby / NOAA
pg. 18, Credit: John Durban / NOAA
pg. 21, Credit: Lance Barrett-Lennard / NOAA
pg. 24, Orca Fluke: © Robin W. Baird

Cover design by Alison Anderson/Blue Peacock Creative
http://bluepeacockcreative.com

Olivia's Pod: An Orca's Tale
Copyright, 2012 by Kurt Meidinger

Published by G8Press
PO Box 8312
Redlands CA 92373
www.G8Press.com

ISBN 13: 978-0-6157-2261-0
ISBN 10: 0-6157-2261-X

Dedicated to my wife, Jill, for her patience and enduring support.

It is a cold, gray November morning in Alaska. I love the cold so much even though it feels like the inside of a freezer. Yes, it is perfect weather. I often breach out of the water to enjoy the freezing rain blowing against my side.

My name is Olivia.

I am an Orca

and this is my family.

We travel as a clan up and down the Pacific coast between Washington state and Alaska.

You can see only four of us in this picture, but our pod consists of twenty related orcas. Some pods have forty family members. Because we are all related, we call ourselves a clan.

That's me on top getting some cool, fresh air through my blowhole. The chubby Orca behind me is my brother, Oscar. He is always bothering me. You can see how he likes to nudge me with his rounded head.

Here is my mom and baby sister, Maria. Isn't my mom beautiful? She is the leader of our pod. Orcas let the oldest female lead. We call her the matriarch.

Sometimes we're called killer whales because we're such great predators. We'll eat almost any kind of mammal that has the misfortune to cross our path.

My favorite prey is sea lions.

Maria prefers sea otters because they are smaller.

Oscar eats anything. He likes sea lions, sea otters, dolphins, and even a swimming moose or deer.

My mom is the best hunter of all. Occasionally, when we're really hungry, she and Aunt Hilda will kill another whale. They crash into it and drown it.

We are also called transient Orcas. That means we're always moving up and down the coast looking for food. Our cousins are called offshore Orcas. That's right, they live far offshore. They don't eat delicious mammals like we do. They only eat fish. How boring!

Here I am swimming happily with Uncle Alvin. Take a look at our curvy, streamlined shape and slick, smooth skin. It helps us move quickly through the water so we're sure to catch our next meal.

Can you see Uncle Alvin's tail? It's called a fluke. It waves up and down instead of sideways like a fish. Our flukes help us dive or ascend quickly to the surface. It's great when you want to breach out of the water for some fresh Arctic air.

Well I have to go now. The rest of my pod is here and they heard about this great area for hunting sea lions. I'm feeling a little hungry too. Let's just hope I get there before Oscar eats them all.

www.ingramcontent.com/pod-product-compliance
Lightning Source LLC
Chambersburg PA
CBHW042102040426
42448CB00002B/108